Chessie System Railroads in West Virginia

compiled by Thomas W. Dixon, Jr.

©
2007
The Chesapeake & Ohio Historical Society, Inc.
P.O. Box 79
Clifton Forge, Va. 24422
1-800-453-COHS
www.cohs.org

Front Cover:

Eastbound Extra 8260 gasps for air exiting the newer (1932) of the two Big Bend Tunnels. At 6,168 feet in lenght Big Bend is the longest on the C&O. The original tunnel - named Great Bend - is located a few feet to the right. Big Bend Tunnel was made famous in legend and lore as the battleground between former slave and drill steel driver John Henry and the steam rock drill. That contest between man and machine supposedly happened in the 1870s when the tunnel was under construction. (Everett N. Young Photo)

Digital Image Production and Book Design
Mac Beard
Copy Editor: Rick Tabb

The Chesapeake & Ohio Historical Society, Inc. is a non-profit organization dedicated to the collection, preservation and dissemination of information about, and preservation and interpretation of the history of the Chesapeake & Ohio Railway, its predecessors and successors. The Society operates a full-service archives staffed professionally, sells a wide variety of models, books and pamphlets. It also publishes pamphlets, full length books such as this and a monthly magazine dealing with all aspects of C&O history.

The Society may be contacted by writing:

The Chesapeake & Ohio Historical Society
P.O. Box 79,
Clifton Forge, VA 24422

or calling toll free 1-800-453-COHS (Monday-Saturday 9am-5pm), or by e-mail at: cohs@cohs.com. The Society maintains a history information Internet site at www.cohs.org, and a full service sales site at www.chessieshop.com.

International Standard Book Number 0-939487-82-9
Library of Congress Control Number 2007923074

TABLE of CONTENTS

Father of Chessie System, President, Chairman and CEO Hays T. Watkins, is shown here with a model of one of the first demonstrator Chessie System units, B&O 1977 at the time the new image was debuted.
(Chessie System Photo, COHS Collection.)

Introduction

Acknowledgements

I am not the author of this book, but its compiler. I wrote only the introduction. The photos and their captions are the work of a few fine railfan photographers whose work apprears on these pages: Everett N. Young, E. Roy Ward, Arthur E. House, James Moseley, E. Sterling Hanger, Jr. and myself. These photos were taken as part of a hobby interest but they have become an important record of a particular period and locale in the history of these three railroads and in American railroading.

During the first years of the C&O and B&O "affiliation" the logos of the two roads were joined in this way and the company was called "C&O/B&O Railroads" on its letterhead.

For over a decade the verdant green hills of West Virginia served as backdrop to diesel locomotives painted in a vibrant yellow powering huge trains of coal and merchandise destined to the industrial centers of America. These locomotives were emblazoned with the initials of three great railroads: the ancient Baltimore & Ohio, mother of American railroads, the Chesapeake & Ohio, long recognized as the "Coal Bin of America," and the short but scenic coal and lumber hauling Western Maryland. This was the period in which the locomotives of these three companies operated together under the name of Chessie System Railroads.

This book looks at the operations of Chessie System in the state of West Virginia beginning in 1972 when the first units arrived, and carries through into the mid-1980s when the much loved Chessie System paint scheme was exchanged for the various liveries of CSX Transportation.

Several books and many magazine articles and videos, have covered the trains of Chessie System, but this book is intended to look at its operation in one defined geographical area. West Virginia was chosen for several reasons. It contained important operations for all three lines, and it was the source of much of their wealth through the transportation of coal from mines that proliferated up and down the valleys and hollows of the "Mountain State." The nature of the operations also required big diesel locomotives or a lot of them to power heavy trains over heavy grades leaving the coal fields.

The southern part of the state was served by the Chesapeake & Ohio's myriad of branches radiating from its main line between its entry in the east from Virginia at the top of Alleghany Mountain to its exit in the west into Kentucky across the Big Sandy River near Huntington. The Baltimore & Ohio had a similar set of lines crossing the northern part of the state from entry at Harpers Ferry, across the state to Parkersburg, up the panhandle to Wheeling, down the Ohio to Huntington, and down through the center of the state to Charleston. The Western Maryland operated generally in some of the same areas as

B&O in Maryland and northeastern West Virginia, tapping similar coal fields and lumber lands.

The nostalgia and culture that associated with railroading in West Virginia also have a particular draw for many of the people who today have an interest in railroading for its historical value, as enthusiasts for its operations, as model hobbyists, or as people who connect it with local history. It is very much like the culture of railroading and mining that is found in Colorado which has infatuated so many people since the hobby of railroad history and modeling first gained maturity.

As background it should be understood that the three railroads in this study were all operating as fully independent lines in 1960. It was just a year or two after that when C&O acquired controlling interest in Baltimore & Ohio, and a few years later that the WM was brought into the picture from its status as a line controlled by B&O. C&O had acquired a reputation as a gold-plated company that was always on top financially, operationally, managerially, and in many other ways. It used its huge and steady income from coal hauling to make itself not only a blue chip investment, but to become a leader in railroad innovation and management, especially in the decades just following the end of World War II.

By the late 1950s C&O was looking for a partner to expand its horizons, and because it could not capture the preferred New York Central, the B&O came under consideration. The B&O was considered a weak railroad financially, but it had a system larger than C&O, and was like it in many ways, not the least of which was a reliance on coal for a large part of its income. Also there was little real overlap in the two systems; they were not largely competitive. But B&O had fallen on bad days and was struggling financially. C&O management decided that it would be advantageous to acquire the line with a view to eventual merger, which was accomplished in 1962. The new system began calling itself C&O/B&O Railroads, using a combination of the C&O for Progress and B&O Capitol Dome logos. At the same time thought was being given as to how the line's new image should be projected in the longer term. As a result Howard Skidmore, C&O's Vice President Public Relations, commissioned a study in 1965 to determine a new name and image for a combined company. The name "Chessie System" was the clear preference in this study.

This was a natural outgrowth of the marvelous success C&O had with the Chessie ad campaign starting in 1933. The cuddly half-asleep kitten supposedly drowsing in air-conditioned comfort on one of C&O's name trains had expanded from just advertising the comforts of passenger travel on C&O to became in effect the very image of the railway itself. This had been bolstered in the public's mind through a concerted, concentrated, and highly imaginative advertising and public relations campaign year after year, supplemented with the ever-growing popularity of the annual Chessie Calendar which C&O issued in monumental quantities. By the 1960s, with passenger traffic in eclipse, Chessie was being used in many ads featuring coal, merchandise traffic, and industrial development. The names "C&O" and "Chessie" had become interchangeable. Chessie is still recognized in advertising history as one of the best loved and, in her day, best known corporate symbols.

But the new name was not immediately adopted. The C&O/B&O logos and name continued during the years when the two companies moved from two distinctly operated entities into more and more consolidations of functions and operations. By the late 1960s motive power and cars had become almost completely interchangeable, and many offices had been consolidated and reorganized, as well as engineering and mechanical functions, as the two roads moved toward a genuine merger.

B&O and C&O both had blue diesels, so as consolidated orders were placed. C&O Enchantment Blue was adopted for both lines, as a large "C&O" or "B&O" replaced spelled-out road names on diesel flanks. Locomotives and cars still carried the logos of each respective lines: "For Progress" on C&O units and cars and the "Capitol Dome" on B&O units and cars. Standards were adopted which mandated the repainting of older units to the new scheme as needed, and many were, but many retained their original livery.

In 1971 Hays T. Watkins became President and Chairman of the combined companies, and decided that the image change was finally needed. Howard Skidmore, still at the public relations helm, asked his creative department, headed by Franklyn Carr, to adopt the Chessie System name and develop a livery and logo to use it. Skidmore was impressed with the bold paint schemes used by western railroads, particularly Santa Fe's Warbonnet scheme, and wanted something similarly eye-catching.

Franklyn Carr's design for the new scheme was inspired, of course, by the classic image of the sleeping Chessie. He simply took the standard design, placed it in a circle, and drew a stylized outline of the kitten. This then formed the uppercase "C" in the words Chessie System. The balance of the name was also portrayed in a very bold, thick font. Skidmore enthusiastically approved Carr's design as did Mr. Watkins and the Board of Directors.

The capital "C" with Chessie's outline was called the "Ches-C," and replaced the C&O For Progress logo wherever it appeared, such as the fronts of locomotives, the sides of freight cars, etc. The full lettering also appeared the sides of locomotives and on the cars as well.

The Locomotives were to borrow a page from the western railroads as well with regard to the body paint, UP's design being the best example. The new Chessie System design featured the body of the locomotive painted in C&O's famous Federal Yellow, on which the Chessie System name was painted in the old Enchantment Blue color. Above the doors along the hood was a vermilion stripe. The space above it, along the skyline of the locomotive's long hood side, extending through the cab and to the top of the short hood (for the newer locomotives) was in blue. The trucks, underbody, and pilot were blue.

This was a radical departure from the subdued blues prevalent on C&O and B&O equipment and from the dull colors used by many other eastern railroads.

By 1973 Western Maryland had been subsumed into Chessie System and its units received the same paint treatment.

The traditional Chessie emblem, which in the mind of many was the unofficial logo of the C&O (right), was stylized by Creative Designer Franklyn Carr of C&O for the new "Ches-C" logo for Chessie System. He simply outlined Chessie in solid blue, leaving her image as a cut-out.

The new paint scheme became the darling of railfan photographers, publicity officials, and everyone connected with the railroads involved. It was a great morale boost for employees, and it had the desired effect on the general public as well. Even the railroad's safety department liked it because of the good visibility the locomotives presented in yards and at grade crossings, in bad weather and good. In all it was a master stroke. As new cars and locomotives were received the new scheme and many older ones were repainted.

In 1980 Chessie System and Seaboard System (itself a combination of the old Atlantic Coast Line, Seaboard Air Line, Louisville & Nashville, Clinchfield, and Georgia) were both put under an overarching holding company called CSX. It was announced at the time that this was just a temporary name and that it would never be used on equipment. The rationale behind the letters was: "C" for Chessie System, "S" for Seaboard System, and the multiplication sign "X" meaning that the two working together would be greater than the whole of each separately.

But by the mid-1980s things had changed and CSX was entrenched. Locomotives and cars were given a new paint scheme featuring the large CSX letters, a scheme which has changed several times down to the present day. The sub-lettering of locomotives and cars to their constituent company ownership was discontinued as the subordinate companies were gradually merged legally into each other and finally into today's CSX Transportation.

Over the twenty years since the repainting into CSX started, all the Chessie locomotives had been repainted and/or retired and none are believed left in service at this writing.

C&O operations in West Virginia in the 1960s were largely unchanged from that which they had been over the previous 40 years, with the exception of a diminishing number and final elimination of passenger trains, and the elimination of local freight business, as was occurring on railroads nationwide. Many stations had been closed by this time or were closed in the period as Less-Than-Carload freight (LCL) disappeared and along with it the need for freight depots and agents. Also by this time Centralized Traffic Control (CTC) signaling had been installed on all major lines and the towers ("cabins" in C&O parlance) had been largely eliminated. The C&O

The Ches-C, in addition to being the stand-alone logo of the line, formed the capital "C" in the full Chessie System name.

and B&O "affiliation" began to look more like a merger in modern terms by 1970, as motive power assignments had been consolidated, schedules integrated, and general operational practices made more uniform.

Initially many C&O units were seen on the B&O but few B&O units on the C&O because of the great need for more and newer locomotives on the B&O at the time of the take-over. By the 1970s motive power had become homogeneous and B&O and C&O locomotives appeared on both railroads as needed. In 1971 passenger operations were taken over by Amtrak, so there was never a Chessie System passenger locomotive or car for revenue service. Numerous passenger cars appeared in Chessie System paint for official use (business cars and roadway inspection, safety instruction, etc.). Of course the Chessie Steam Special ran a huge excursion train with an ex-Reading Railroad 4-8-4 painted in Chessie Colors (followed later by ex-C&O 4-8-4 No. 614 painted less garishly.)

During the early Chessie era locomotives congregated principally at Hinton, Handley, and Huntington on the C&O mainline, much as in the past. It was only during the early CSX days that the first two were essentially eliminated as locomotive terminals. On branch lines Chessie units could be seen at Peach Creek for the Logan fields, and at Danville, Elk Run Junction, Raleigh (Beckley), and Quinnimont, again not much different from the past. But in the decade and a half that followed these terminals would gradually decline in importance and viability as the pattern of traffic changed. Likewise B&O's locomotive terminals remained fairly static, a principal location being Grafton, which, taken in context, is really very much a mirror of Hinton on the C&O, as is Cumberland (Maryland) on B&O is comparable to Huntington on the C&O.

Although some GP9s were repainted Chessie colors very early and they appeared on West Virginia lines, most of these older units were left until retirement in their old schemes. But as new orders for locomotives arrived, they came, of course, in Chessie paint.

The first debut of the scheme in West Virginia was on November 18, 1972, when GP40-2s painted in the new livery powered five special Amtrak passenger trains to White Sulphur Springs. Only weeks after this date the new U30B General Electric units were received in Chessie paint and went into use in West Virginia. As other new units arrived they very often received assignments on the coal lines of West Virginia. In the 1972-1978 period the most common occurrence was to see a set of mixed paint scheme units on trains, but as time passed the Chessie scheme became predominant, both because older units were repainted and because many older units were retired.

By the end of the Chessie era in West Virginia and the arrival of CSX Transportation, the metamorphosis of

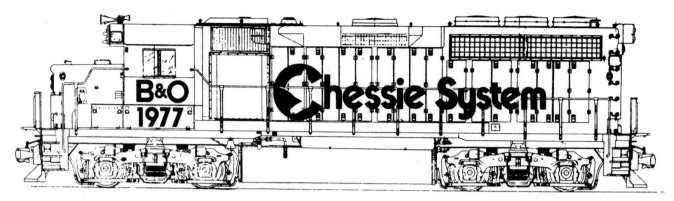

As applied to locomotives, the new lettering usually covered most of the long hood. Part of the PR Department's test of the new name and logo was to see if people failed to understand the "Ches-C" and thought the name was "Hessie System," almost everyone understood the nuance of the design, and it became very popular.

the old C&O, B&O, and WM lines accelerated. The last station buildings, even some which had been saved to be used by company forces, were largely eliminated, coal operations were originating in very large scale treatment plans and mines, ever larger in capacity and smaller in number, many branches were abandoned or dormant because of mine closings, and almost all yard operations had been reduced to bare minimums or eliminated.

Unit coal trains moving from one mine directly to the customer eliminated the need for most en route handing. Bigger locomotives meant fewer units; bigger cars meant fewer trains; fewer mines and fewer customers meant bigger trains, run on demand. The new locomotives required little in-service maintenance and even held enough fuel so that they had to be refueled only at the end-points of very long runs, thus completely eliminating the need for refueling terminals.

At about the beginning of the Chessie System period, the Alleghany Subdivision main line underwent some major changes. The West Virginia portion of the C&O main line was singled-tracked near Talcott, which included the elimination of the old bore at Big Bend Tunnel. Other second track segments were taken up as well on the New River Subdivision, as traffic appeared to be on a more or less steady decline. Numerous branches became inactive or were completely abandoned as the nature of coal mining changed. On the B&O the largest change was abandonment of a large segment of the old St. Louis line between Grafton and Parkersburg, a line which, ironically, had received a major upgrade just a few years before. Some of the old Coal & Coke Line to Charleston was also abandoned. But by the end of the era and the beginning of CSXT traffic was rebounding.

During the Chessie System era the constituent railroads really became an operational whole. Central dispatching and central-remote management became possible through technological advances.

This book is intended as a remembrance of the decade and a half when these bright, shiny, flashy locomotives and cars traversed the mountains and valleys of West Virginia hauling merchandise and coal. The scope of the book is geographically limited exclusively to lines in West Virginia. It is an album of photos more than anything else, and a fond remembrance of a great era in railroading. For detailed data on locomotives and cars one can find very adequate treatment in Morning Sun Publishing's *Chessie System Color Guide to Freight Equipment*, and for locomotives, TLC Publishing's *Chessie System Diesel Locomotives*.

Thomas W. Dixon, Jr., President, C&OHS
Lynchburg, Va., March 2007

The Chessie System Railroads in West Virginia

Early in their careers, SD50s 8575 and 8572 skirt the placid Greenbrier River at Wolf Creek. The end of this loaded eastbound is still on the Riffe scales, but soon the engineer will hear the message that "Riffe scale is clear," his cue to resume track speed. April 7, 1984. (Everett N. Young photo)

Chapter One

The Chesapeake & Ohio

The C&O's main line in West Virginia runs from Tuckahoe, just on the western side of Alleghany Tunnel, down the Greenbrier River to its junction with the New River at Hinton, always a major division point for the railway. This portion of the line was about 2/3rds of the Alleghany Subdivision, running from Clifton Forge, Va. to Hinton. From Hinton the line follows the New River through its famous gorge to its junction with the Gauley River, then along the Kanawha River to the state capital at Charleston, thence to Huntington. At Huntington the B&O's Ohio River line joined from Parkersburg. A few miles west of Huntington the C&O crossed the Big Sandy River into Kentucky. Of course there were scores of branch lines tapping the still rich coal fields north, but primarily south of the main line.

(See the 1978 Chessie System map on page 34-35.)

SD50s 8553 and 8566 coupled to U30B 8205 and GP40 4036 pick up speed with a 61-car ore train bound for Ashland, Ky. The arrival of an infrequent ore boat at Baltimore resulted in a flurry of ore trains for a few days until the shipment was moved. A hopper door slightly ajar or a hole in the side of a car meant taconite pellets bouncing off the roadbed like marbles. April 8, 1984. (Everett N. Young photo)

C&O GP40 3790 leads 4402, 4236 and 8233 west on No. 93 at Tuckahoe. The train is just out of Alleghany Tunnel and picking up speed. June 1, 1985. (Everett N. Young photo)

The long pull nearly over, Extra 3885 East rounds the big curve at Tuckahoe. It has been 123 miles of constant 0.56 percent grade from Whitcomb where the main line leaves the Greenbrier River for Howards Creek. Sept. 29, 1985. (Everett N. Young Photo)

When the General Motors Executives traveled to C&O's Greenbrier Hotel in White Sulphur Springs, W. Va., in November 1972 they could no longer come by C&O special train, so specials were arranged with the new Amtrak. On the night before arrival of the five special all-sleeper trains C&O placed brand new B&O GP40-2 No. 1977 in Chessie Paint Scheme (commemorating 150 years of the B&O) and GM-50, B&O's commemorative unit praising the 50'" Anniversary of EMD, on display at the depot, flood-lit at night. These two photos show that great scene. This was the debut of the Chessie paint scheme for the GM and C&O officials. November 15, 1972. (Both photos T. W. Dixon, Jr.)

C&O GP40-2s 4175 and 4165, just out of the EMD plant, lead Union Pacific E9Bs (for power and steam heat), and a huge 18 car all sleeper train arriving at White Sulphur Springs with General Motors executives. The new Amtrak put together over 100 sleeping cars from their recently acquired fleet. This train is almost all UP and the first to arrive that foggy morning of November 11, 1972. (T. W. Dixon, Jr. Photo)

Even after C&O gave up its passenger operations to Amtrak, occasionally a special train was operated into White Sulphur Springs, reminiscent of the old times. Here B&O GP40-2 No. 4444 has a train of Chessle System business cars at the White Sulphur Springs depot the night of Sept. 9, 1982 handling a meeting of the Business Government Relations Council. The second photo shows the rear of the train. (Both photos Tod Hanger)

GP40-2 #4172 leads two other Chessie units with an eastbound coal train through White Sulphur Springs, W.Va., in July 1985. (Jim Moseley Photo)

From the I-64 bridge west of White Sulphur Springs, B30-7s 8272 and 8266 struggle east at Harts Run. Two SD40s pushing will cut off at Alleghany. Jan. 29, 1983 (Everett N. Young Photo)

An eastbound coal train headed by B&O #8242 is about to leave Ronceverte, W.Va. in this October 1988 picture. Note the C&O coaling tower and the cantilever signal bridge in the background. (Photo Jim Moseley)

At the beginning of the diesel age, pushers on eastbound coal trains disappeared. By the early 1980s it was apparent that a pusher crew on the most severe portion of the Alleghany grade could eliminate the need for four or five units per coal train over the whole subdivision. SD40s 7527 and 7502 push through Ronveverte having coupled on just west of town. The well-used track to the right of the train is a 12,000-foot signaled siding. The station still has a train order signal although no operator. Jan. 30, 1983 . (Everett N. Young Photo)

We see C&O Extra 8260 grinding out of Manns Tunnel on its methodical march east. Three tunnels were necessary at Fort Spring to avoid sharp bends in the Greenbrier River: Second Creek, Fort Spring, and Manns. Sept. 29, 1985. (Everett N. Young Photo)

C&O GP7 5834 with work train westbound at Ft. Spring, W. Va. In Feb. 1976. This old GP9 was one of the older units to receive Chessie paint scheme. It was finally retired ten years after this photo and scrapped. (T. W. Dixon, Jr. Photo)

Chessie 4233, 7602, 2301 and 4376 muscle a 125-car eastbound drag out of Manns Tunnel at Fort Spring. The two lunar lights on the westbound block signal are the Train Defect Indicator that works in conjunction with the Defective Equipment Detector. Although this light is for westbounds, both lights illuminated continuously mean no defect. If this eastbound receives a flashing indication from the Train Defect Indicator at Ronceverte, he must stop and determine the cause. This installation has been replaced with audible detectors at various other locations. Oct. 10, 1980. (Everett N. Young Photo)

C&O SD9-40 No. 7530 makes good speed emerging eastbound from Mann's Tunnel at Ft. Spring, W. Va. with a manifest freight in June 1977, the locomotive shining in Chessie paint. (T. W. Dixon, Jr. Photo)

Extra 8260 marches east through Alderson on Track 2. The restored depot serves as a flag stop for Amtrak's tri-weekly *Cardinal*. Sept. 29, 1985. (Everett N. Young Photo)

Chessie SD50s 8593 and 8563 are in their prime as they roll by the AD Cabin crossovers at Alderson. This 156-car drag will get a pusher at Ronceverte. June 1, 1985. (Everett N. Young Photo)

Westbound in the late evening with empty coal cars at AD Cabin, just west of Alderson, W. Va. C&O SD40 No. 7530 in bright clean Chessie paint leads four other units in C&O blue in August 1976. (T. W. Dixon, J. Photo)

The Chessie Safety Express is westbound at Alderson, W.Va., in October, 1981. C&O 4-8-4 No. 614 was assisted across the Alleghany grade by two diesels, led by C&O B30-7 8290. (Photo by Art House)

Eastbound coal behind mixed GM and GE power exits Big Bend Tunnel, Talcott, W.Va., October, 1981. B&O GP-35 3724 heads the train. (Photo by Art House)

Eastbound Extra 8260 gasps for air exiting the newer (1932) of the two Big Bend Tunnels. At 6,168 feet Big Bend is the longest on the C&O. The original tunnel - named Great Bend - is located a few feet to the right. Big Bend Tunnel was made famous in legend and lore as the battleground between former slave and drill steel driver John Henry and the steam rock drill. That contest between man and machine supposedly happened in the 1870s when the tunnel was under construction. (Everett N. Young Photo)

Eastbound grain behind C&O GP40-2 No. 4286 ascends the grade to Big Bend Tunnel between Hinton and Hilldale, W.Va., in October, 1981. (Photo by Art House)

Extra 4233 East is looking at the signal at MX Cabin awaiting departure from Hinton. Loaded coal trains were forwarded through town to Avis Yard located between the depot and MX Cabin. In the Chessie System era, MX was the demarcation line between the West Virginia Division and the Virginia Division. Oct. 10, 1980. (Everett N. Young Photo)

Side-lit by a low sun on a cold day in January 1977 C&O U-30B No. 8226 and three other units in C&O blue are leaving Hinton, W. Va. eastbound with a fast freight train. Although GE units were common on the Alleghany Subdivision the crews liked them far less than EMD units, which they said were easier riders and less slippery. (T. W. Dixon, J. Photo)

Chessie C&O #8294, GE B30-7 works past the ex C&O station at Hinton W.Va., in October 1984. The station still survives as an Amtrak stop. (Jim Moseley Photo)

Chessie System, C&O, GE B30-7 #8294 works the yard at Hinton, W.Va., past some still surviving C&O buildings in October 1984. (Jim Moseley Photo)

Parked in front of the Hinton, W. Va. yard office in October 1975, a brace of units is ready for service On October 18, 1975, Chessie paint scheme U30B No. 8223 facing the camera, with three C&O blue in units coupled. (T. W. Dixon, Jr. Photo)

Showing in brilliant sun the changing face of the C&O, GP9 5991 is in the bright Chessie paint while the accompanying units display the Big-C&O scheme and the original Futura Demibold lettering. Hinton, W. Va., March 1977. (T. W. Dixon, Jr. Photo)

The Hinton engine terminal was a good pace to find motive power in the steam, early diesel, or Chessie System days. Here GP40-2 No. 4182 and a mate pause with other locomotives awaiting assignments on the Alleghany or New River Subdivisions in January 1977. (T. W. Dixon, Jr. Photo)

Ex-Reading 4-8-4 2101, the *Chessie Steam Special's* power, is being serviced at Hinton during the train's layover on an October, 1978, Huntington-Hinton-Huntington turn. (Photo by Art House)

B&O GP40-2 No. 4107 and three other units take a coal train east passing MD Cabin at Meadow Creek, W. Va. In April 1976. (T. W. Dixon, Jr. Photo)

Four big Geeps have the "G&E Shifter" in tow heading for the Lady H Coal Co. Quinwood 2 Mine. Besides the 31 empty hoppers on this Sunday trip, the shifter has four loads of cleaner coal that will be dumped and cleaned. The Greenbrier & Eastern Railroad was conveyed to the Nicholas, Fayette & Greenbrier Railroad, a joint C&O and New York Central operation, in 1932. This train will proceed over newer trackage that extended into Nicholas County during World War II. Oct. 25, 1986. (Everett N. Young Photo)

Late in the day, a westbound led by SD35 7430 pauses at Quinnimont to set off empty hoppers for the "Piney Shifter" to take up to Raleigh. Sept. 10, 1977. (Everett N. Young Photo)

Five big Geeps pull by the Quinnimont yard office with the "Piney Shifter" out of Raleigh Yard. QN Cabin was the last surviving example of the tower-depot combination that once dotted the C&O main line. By October 26, 1980 this structure was an anachronism. A modern photo copier sat next to a window that still had coal dust in the sills put there by passing steam locomotives. A few years after this photo, QN cabin was demolished. (Everett N. Young Photo)

Eastbound coal behind B&O GP-40 No. 4016 passes the Prince, W.Va. passenger depot and NI Cabin (on left), August, 1983. (Photo by Art House.)

B&O GP40-2 #4119 is passing by the ex-C&O station at Prince W.Va. with a westbound empty hopper train in this October, 1981 scene. Note the small unusual Chessie on the nose. (Photo Jim Moseley)

The "Piney Shifter" behind five Geeps rolls over the New River near Prince. This train has delivered coal loads to Quinnimont Yard and is returning to Raleigh Yard near Beckley with 140 empty hoppers. If needed, a second Piney job will run at night. October 26, 1980. (Everett N. Young Photo)

Three GE U30Bs - 8211, 8213 and 8202 - with GP38 3854 move an eastbound manifest freight through Thurmond on June 30, 1974. Post office patrons needed to observe both ways before stepping out onto the narrow sidewalk that served as Thurmond's "Main Street." (Everett N. Young Photo)

Westbound manifest No. 93 waits at Thurmond depot for an eastbound to come off single track. Ninety three had no less than seven of the new SD50s plus an older SD40. Even on overcast days, the appealing Chessie paint scheme brightens the picture. It's easy to understand why this scheme was a favorite among railfans and modellers. Jan. 7, 1985. (Everett N. Young Photo)

A Chessie, C&O, GP35 & 3529 and an assortment of other C&O locomotives stand ready for duty outside the engine house at Thurmond, W.Va., in October 1981. (Photo Jim Moseley)

Chessie C&O, GE B30-7 #8292 leads another B30-7 west with a hopper train deep in the New River Gorge at Sewell, W.Va., in April 1983. (Photo Jim Moseley)

Raleigh Yard near Beckley was the focal point of mine runs in the Winding Gulf Field. The yard hangs over a 1.3 percent grade in both directions, the summit of which is to the left of the coal dock. Oct. 10, 1980. (Everett N. Young Photo)

Three Chessie Geeps have supplied empty hoppers to the Skelton Mine on the north side of Beckley and will now commence to gather their loads to the main line of the Piney River & Paint Creek Subdivision on the right. The empty covered hopper came from an explosives dealer at Cranberry where the bulk ammonia nitrate was unloaded. Sept. 28, 1985. (Everett N. Young Photo)

Five big Geeps roll by Beckley Junction with the "Beckley Mine Man" from out near Glen Daniels. Until the 1960s, a small train order office was located here. August 27, 1985. (Everett N. Young Photo)

Two unidentified Chessie units pull a westbound hopper train over the New River at Hawks Nest, W.Va., in October 1981. (Photo Jim Moseley)

The "East Pickup" passes the "Gauley Shifter" as it stashes its loads in the center siding at Gauley, near wher the New and Gualey Rivers form the Kanawha. March 24, 1984. (Everett N. Young Photo)

An eastbound coal train behind GP40-2 4183, U23B 2312 and GP9 6192 arrives at Handley Yard on Aug. 19, 1974. Besides trains from Russell, road crews from Peach Creek also terminated at Handley. (Everett N. Young Photo)

Eastbound coal behind B&O GP-40 no. 4016 passes the Prince, W.V. passenger depot and NI Cabin (on left), August, 1983. (Photo by Art House.)

The "Gauley Shifter" crosses the Gauley River at Belva. One small tipple at Vaughan loaded only a few cars each month making a move past Belva rather infrequent. In the 1990s, the line was extended above Vaughan to serve the Fola Mine under private ownership. The rest of the track was upgraded to handle larger locomotives and cars. Past Belva, the track became the Vaughan Railroad. A new connection gave Conrail access to the mine also. March 24, 1984. (Everett N. Young Photo)

After taking loads to the main line center siding, the "Gauley Shifter" returns to K&M Junction yard with empty hoppers. Engines other than the smaller Geeps were restricted from the branch which would later be beefed up to handle the big six-axle AC units. March 24, 1984. (Everett N. Young Photo)

In addition to serving coal tipples, the "Gauley Shifter" also worked the interchange at Gauley Bridge between C&O and Conrail. GP30 3029 is heading back across the Gauley River on Conrail track to the C&O's small K&M Junction yard. The main line of Conrail's West Virginia Secondary is on the other side of the depot. Conrail is former New York Central whose predecessor here was the Kanawha & Michigan Railway. March 24, 1984. (Everett N. Young Photo)

SD40 7515 and GP38 3854 skirt the Kanawha River at Eagle with the "East Pickup." Eagle is two miles east of Montgomery. March 24, 1984. (Everett N. Young Photo)

The "East Pickup" behind almost-new SD50 8566 is stopped at Chelyan on Track 1. Former C&O Greenbrier 614-T will soon over-take. The 4-8-4 was utilized for a month to obtain data for Ross Rowland's ACE 3000 coal-fired locomotive of the future. January 7, 1985. (Everett N. Young Photo)

This view of the Danville engine terminal from the US 119 bridge offers a variety of locomotives that can't be seen today. A B&O and C&O GP9, a C&O SD35 and SD40, plus a GE B30-7. Today no locomotives are serviced at any of CSXT's coal field yards except Grafton. Aug. 13, 1983. (Everett N. Young Photo)

A westbound coal train digs in for the pull at Scary. Commencing at St. Albans, this train faces approximately eight miles of 0.30 percent grade leading out of the Kanawha River valley. In steam days, this was enough to warrant a Mikado pusher. The important spur leading north to the coal-fired John Amos power plant is just to the left of this view. July 31, 1983. (Everett N. Young Photo)

A westbound coal train behind SD40 7532 and Geeps 6616, 5883 and 6595 approaches Barboursville, location of weigh-in-motion scales. The track on the right leads to the east leg of the wye junction with the Logan Subdivision. July 31, 1983. (Everett N. Young Photo)

C&O SD40 7530 sits on the Peach Creek, W. Va. yard In company with C&O blue units and many cars in this October 1977 scene at one of C&O's major coal marshalling yards throughout the 20th Century. (T. W. Dixon, Jr. Photo)

Parked on the engine terminal lead at Peach Creek are two of C&O's relatively rare GE U30C models. C&O ordered 13 U30Cs; 3300-3303 comprised the first order and 3304-3313 the second. On the first order - 3301 in this view - the widening of the hood at the radiator is abrupt and only the center area is raised. On 3305 the entire roof in the radiator area is raised, and the width flaired on the side. April 30, 1978. (Everett N. Young Photo)

C&O bay window caboose 904102 was part of a 66-car order built by Fruit Growers Express in 1980. They were the last cabooses ordered for the C&O, and the only bay-window type owned. By February 1990 when photographed at Peach Creek Yard, cabooses had been eliminated on through freights. Even these most modern of cabs had been relegated to local and mine run service where long back-up moves were required. (Everett N. Young Photo)

The "Elk Creek shifter" approaches FD Cabin in Logan having just departed the Peach Creek Empty Yard. Elk Creek Subdivision branched off the Logan Subdivision at Wylo, 19 miles up the Guyandotte River. Island Creek Coal Co. had a large preparation plant there that warranted a shifter each day. Jan. 10, 1986 (Everett N. Young Photo)

Gene Huddleston put Rum Junction on the railfan map with his description of a Mallet-powered mine run stopping and then proceeding up the branch in 1952. Rum Junction is still an important place in the Logan District. A shifter behind 7575, 2323 and 4185 has 35 loads of cleaner coal for Amherst Coal's MacGregor preparation plant at the head of the hollow. Three units will have their work cut out for the grade will reach 2.37 percent. May 10, 1983. (Everett N. Young Photo)

B&O 4159 and C&O 3867 hustle an eastbound "Buffalo Backup" past Elkay Mining's tipple at Earling. The empty hoppers will be distributed to the several tipples up Buffalo Creek east of Man. May 10, 1983. (Everett N. Young Photo)

SD50 8626 has the "Buffalo Lundale" shifter with 35 empties eastbound at Taplin. Taplin is a five-car storage yard just west of Man. In later years it served as a holding location for new American Car & Foundry covered hoppers manufactured at Huntington. In this February 1986 view, old Fruit Growers Express reefers are in storage. The track to the right of the train is the passing siding. The spur leading off to the right served a small tipple. (Everett N. Young Photo)

The "Elk Creek shifter" approaches FD Cabin in Logan having just departed the Peach Creek Empty Yard. Elk Creek Subdivision branched off the Logan Subdivision at Wylo, 19 miles up the Guyandotte River. Island Creek Coal Co. had a large preparation plant there that warranted a shifter each day. Jan. 10, 1986. (Everett N. Young Photo)

Extra 7532 west was crossed over at Scott Depot and is almost to the summit at Teays. July 31, 1983. (Everett N. Young Photo)

SD35 7428 hustles west at Tamcliff with 16 loads picked up at West Gilbert tipple. At Gilbert the C&O met the Virginian Ry. C&O had trackage rights for two miles to reach Gilbert Yard where interchange was formally made. May 10, 1983. (Everett N. Young Photo)

During the Chessie era, the railroad's engineering department was headquartered in Huntington. The three-car roadway inspection was kept at the ready at the C&O passenger station. The last car - RI-2 - was a glass end observation car converted from a 1942 ACF coach. It is now numbered CSXT TGC-2 and called a Track Geometry Car. May 29, 1978. (Everett N. Young Photo)

This little General Electric shop goat shuffled dead locomotives around the Huntington Locomotive Shop from 1917 until it was retired in the 1990s. The significance of number 18742 is anyone's guess. The unit was powered by storage batteries. June 27, 1980s. (Everett N. Young Photo)

No. 91 was C&O's most important main line westbound manifest freight, but it didn't need all 12 of these engines to get it over the road. Fabric is being installed under the roadbed of track 2 at KV Cabin in Kenova. Aug. 22, 1986. (Everett N. Young Photo)

A fast moving westbound coal train behind a GP40-2, GP35, GP30 and GP9 stirs up dust passing KV Cabin at Kenova, WV, on May 13, 1979. KV controlled the crossing with N&W's branch to the barge terminals along the river. Won't see four distinct locomotive models very often on a train these days. (Everett N. Young Photo)

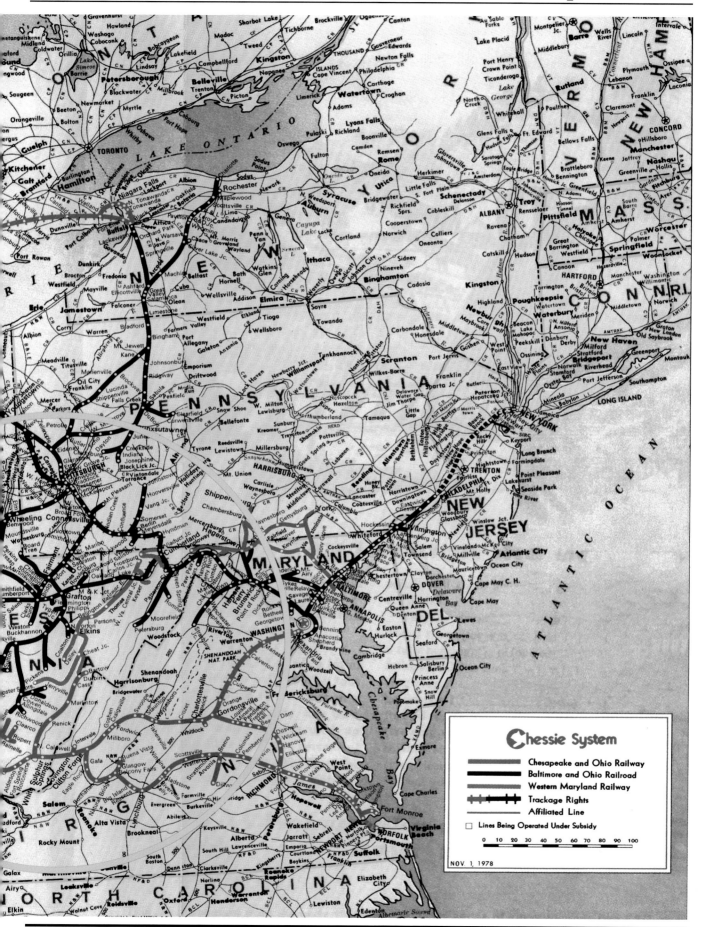

The *St. Louis Trailer Jet* is westbound on B&O main line at Rowlesburg, W.V. in October, 1979. SD-35 7411 leads.
(Photo by Art House)

Chapter Two

The Baltimore & Ohio

The B&O entered West Virginia just west of Oakland, Maryland, not too far west of the line's major yard, terminal, and shop town of Cumberland, Maryland. The old St. Louis line then ran roughly directly west across the state to Parkesburg, where it crossed the River into Ohio. Grafton was a major division point that was in character much like Hinton on the C&O, and from that point a line ran south through the center of the state to Charleston, where connection was made with the C&O. Another line extended north from Parkersburg along the West Virginia side of the Ohio River to Wheeling where lines crossed out of West Virginia east into Pennsylvania and west into Ohio. Like the C&O, the B&O had many coal branches and operations, in this case tapping the coal reaches of the northern portion of the state.

(See the 1978 Chessie System map on page 34-35.)

The local freight off the Green Spring Branch works at the Green Spring station. (E. Roy Ward photo)

An eastbound coal drag fresh off the 17-mile grade rolls by the West Keyser tower. April 4, 1981. (E. Roy Ward photo)

Road power eases out of engine terminal at Keyser Yard to back onto an eastbound coal train. March 19, 1977. (E. Roy Ward photo)

A B&O eastbound whines down the 17-mile grade as a WM "Henry Turn" just arrived at Beryl, W. Va., watches. March 19, 1977. (E. Roy Ward photo)

A B&O westbound makes a run for the 17-mile grade as it passes the Westvaco Paper Mill at Luke, Maryland, on August 15, 1976. The WM Thomas S.D. main line crosses the river here and goes through the paper mill. (E. Roy Ward photo)

GP40 3739 with seven other four-axle units is stopped at Hopemont with freight GW97. Gateway 97 was the premier B&O westbound freight over the Cumberland West End and Monongah Division in West Virginia. It originated at Philadelphia and terminated, as the name implied, in East St. Louis, Ill. Sept. 20, 1980. (Everett N. Young Photo)

This Chessie System, C&O SD50 #8555 was only a few weeks old when photographed pushing a coal train up Cranberry grade near Amblersburg, W. Va., in March, 1984. (Photo Jim Moseley)

ABOVE: M&K Jct. at Rowlesburg served as a base for helpers shoving westbounds up the Cheat River grade and eastbounds up Hardman and Cranberry grades. In steam, 27 2-8-8-0 Mallets were required. F-7s replaced steam, and four unit sets of SD35s came after that. On this Oct. 6, 1979 eleven SD35s are present including one lettered for Western Maryland. (Everett N. Young Photo)

LEFT: An eastbound coal drag slowly climbs Cranberry grade as helpers return west at Amblersburg, W. Va., on May 16, 1984. (E. Roy Ward photo)

SD40-2 7616 leads a GP40-2 and a SD35 on freight WI35 at M&K Junction. Willard 35 originated at Cumberland and ran west via Clarksburg, Brooklyn Junction, Benwood Junction and Newark, Oh., to the big classification yard at Willard, Oh. M&K was also the terminal for the mine run that worked the Morgantown & Kingwood branch down the Cheat River. Oct. 7, 1979. (Everett N. Young Photo)

B&O 4298, 6650, 6955 and 5631 drop east down Cheat River grade into Rowlesburg with freight No. 88. No. 88 was B&O's priority eastbound freight through West Virginia. It originated at East St. Louis and terminated in Philadelphia. On this Oct. 7, 1979 morning, 88 has 111 cars and will soon be stopping at M&K Junction for a pusher. (Everett N. Young Photo)

B&O freight No. 88 (See previous page.) passes the small depot building at Rowelsburg, October, 7, 1979. (Everett N. Young photo)

BOTTOM: GP40-2 4219 and GP40 4094 have eastbound freight OV34 at Gallipolis Ferry on July 15, 1986. Ohio Valley 34 and its counterpart OV33 operated between Huntington, W. Va., and Pittsburgh, Pa. These trains reclassified at Parkersburg and Benwood Junction yard near Wheeling. They also worked Brooklyn Junction (New Martinsville), and Washington, Pa. OV34 is setting off 12 tank cars for Stauffer Chemical, one of the many such plants along the Ohio River Subdivision. (Everett N. Young Photo)

Chessie Sytem, C&O SD50 #8562 and 8564 preparing to push a coal train out of Rowlesburg, W. Va., in March, 1984. The units were less than two months old. (Jim Moseley Photo)

SD35 7438 has been added to the five-unit lash-up on WI35. In the gathering darkness the heavy westbound freight accelerates across the Cheat River bridge. WI35 was a lower priority freight. It has set off coal empties and picked up coal loads. A four-unit set of SD35s will assist up to Blaser. The through truss bridge will be washed out by the catastrophic floods of November 1985 and replaced by a single track deck-girder bridge. Oct. 6, 1979. (Everett N. Young Photo)

Four SD35s on a westbound light helper through Newburg, W. Va. on May 7, 1977. SD35's held down helper assignments through the 1970's but were eventually replaced by SD50s. (E. Roy Ward photo)

B&O SD50 No. 8585 West brings a train down grade past Hardman Tower on September 14, 1985. (E. Roy Ward photo)

GP40-2s 4145, 4303 and 4188 speed westbound SLTT, the St. Louis Trailer Train, into Grafton yard. Following a 20 minute early afternoon crew change, SLTT will be on her way toward Parkersburg with 58 piggybacks. Originating at Philadelphia, SLTT picked up a Baltimore and will set off and pick up at Cincinnati. May 24, 1980. (Everett N. Young Photo)

Grafton, W. Va., showing "D Tower" and the engine terminal. This is also the junction with the Fairmont S.D. and the Parkersburg S.D. (E. Roy Ward photo)

A brace of four units including two in standard Chessie paint, one in old blue colors, and the famous Gold GM50 unit runs around a Chessie Special at Grafton, W. Va. on September 4, 1983. (E. Roy Ward photo)

A Buckhannon Turn leaves Grafton, W. Va. It will use the Parkersburg S.D. for a mile before swinging onto the Cowen S.D. at Berkley Run Junction. September 4, 1983. (E. Roy Ward photo)

On December 14, 1986, a Detroit Edison unit train rolls through Fairmont, W. Va., and will head down the Fairmont S.D. to Grafton. (E. Roy Ward photo)

RIGHT: Nose of B&O GP40-2 No.4243 Westbound crosses the Ohio River bridge over top of the Ohio River S.D. S X TOWER controlled the entrance to the lower yard and the connection to the Parkersburg S.D. and upper yard. (E. Roy Ward photo)

Chessie 7546, 7407 and 7418 roll under the I-79 bridge at Coger. The Grafton-bound drag will pick up three SD35 pushers at Burnsville for the steep climb to Abbot. Oct. 23, 1986. (Everett N. Young Photo

B&O CP40-2 No. 4034 East has coal in tow as it ascends to Knight Tunnel and on to Grafton on September 12, 1984. (Cowen S.D.) (E. Roy Ward photo)

Western Maryland SD40 7546 with B&O SD35s 7407 and 7418 lead an eastbound 83-car drag at Rollyson on B&O's Cowen Subdivision. Oct. 23, 1986. (Everett N. Young Photo)

The helper and rear end (Buckhannon Turn) crew gets their running orders off Operator Debbie Waters at Berryburg Junction on September 4, 1983. Berryburg Junction was the west end of CTC on the Cowen S.D. at the time but was later extended to Hampton Junction. (E. Roy Ward photo)

B&O GP35s 3513 and 3508 lead 3774 and 5609 at Buckhannon on March 26, 1976. Eastbound Second Class freight No. 48 had departed Cowen before daylight and now has 114 coal loads for Grafton. (Everett N. Young Photo)

B&O GP9 6567 with Seaboard SD40-2 8037 and WM GP40 3796 await a call at Cowen engine terminal. In the background is the car shop where the derrick crane on the left is undergoing a rebuild. The SD35s of the Burnsville helper set have been serviced. Four SD35s will soon depart light for Erbacon to pick up a coal train. October 24, 1986 (Everett N. Young Photo)

One of B&Os uncommon SD9s, No. 1840, was the assigned switcher at the Cowen, W. Va., yard. June 20, 1975. (E. Roy Ward photo)

MIDDLE: The B&O "District Run" passes the Point Pleasant depot westbound behind C&O GP38 3886. When needed (usually once a week), a C&O crew would be taxied out of Columbus to use this power to take materials to the Kyger Creek power plant on former C&O trackage across the Ohio River. Chessie would utilize the Conrail bridge between Point Pleasant and Kanauga, Ohio. April 7, 1986. (Everett N. Young Photo)

An eastbound coal drag out of Cowen drifts down grade near Erbacon, W. Va. (E. Roy Ward photo)

B&O GP40-2s 4147, 4327 and 4136 idle with a train of empties at Camden-On-Gauley amidst blazing fall colors. Soon two crews will arrive to take this train over the 29-mile Strouds Creek & Muddelty Subdivision. Oct. 24, 1986 (Everett N. Young Photo)

The 2:30 PM "Scram" crew (Strouds Creek & Muddelty Subdivision mine run) have registered on duty in the tiny Allingdale depot. The headlight comes on, and now they move south (railroad west) on the B&O's Richwood Subdivision. After plucking a B&O "wagon top" caboose off the siding, C&O 4090 with 4230 and 4298 will become the helpers heading up the "Scram." Oct. 24, 1986. (Everett N. Young Photo)

B&O 4147, 4327 and 4136 slowly wind their way over the former Strouds Creek & Muddelty Railroad which was leased and operated by the B&O. With the aid of three more 40s on the rear, the 140 empty hoppers will be deposited at three tipples this day as far west as the outskirts of Summersville. Oct. 24, 1986. (Everett N. Young Photo)

Chessie GP40-2s 4107-4153 make up westbound Second Class freight No. 65 at Gassaway. The crew will soon depart on a Monday, Wednesday, Friday schedule to Charleston that will bring them back the following day on eastbound No. 62. June 4, 1976. (Everett N. Young Photo)

A local works at Brooklyn Junction, the junction between the Ohio River S.D. and Short Line S.D. to Clarksburg. May 9, 1986. (E. Roy Ward photo)

Engines laying over at Parkersburg engine terminal. May 9, 1986. (E. Roy Ward photo)

B&O GP40-2 No. 4141 East is changing crews at OB Tower in Parkersburg, W. Va.., on June 1, 1980. (E. Roy Ward photo)

B&O GP40-2 No. 4243 running as an extra heads west across the Ohio River bridge at Parkersburg, W. Va., on June 1, 1980. (Parkersburg S.D.) (E. Roy Ward photo)

Two blue B&O units spliced by a Chessie unit with caboose run light down the Cowen S.D. at Pleasant Creek, W. Va. June 28, 1981. (E. Roy Ward photo)

On September 16, 1984, a *Chessie Special* fan trip leaves Elkins on its return trip to Grafton on the Belington S.D. These trips were run in conjunction with the Grafton Railroad Festival weekend. (E. Roy Ward photo)

Chapter Three

The Western Maryland

The third and smallest of the Chessie System railroads in its overall size and in West Virginia operations was Western Maryland. It crossed into the state at a point near Luke, Maryland, and ran down the east-central portion of the state to Elkins, its major division point and terminal in West Virginia. It connected with B&O at Elkins and Keyser and with the C&O's Greenbrier branch at Durbin. As both C&O and B&O, WM also primarily hauled coal with some vestige of the great lumber business which had been much of the reason it and its predecessors had been built in the area.

(See the 1978 Chessie System map on page 34-35.)

The Bayard turnaround working its way up the 3+% Blackfork grade in the Blackwater Canyon. The headlight of the helper engine is visible through the trees down the canyon. Up to 15 engines were used to get tonnage up the canyon. (E. Roy Ward photo)

A Bayard switcher working uphill on the Stoney River S.D. near Douglas, W. Va., with coal for the Mt. Storm power plant. May 12, 1978. (E. Roy Ward photo)

A Bayard switcher, with coal for Mt. Storm power plant is climbing out of the Potomac Valley on the Stony River S.D. Normal operation was to have the caboose on the head end and a helper on the rear. May 12, 1978. (E. Roy Ward photo)

A Bayard switcher has just pulled loads off the Elk Run mine spur to the left and has run around them to return to Bayard, W. Va. (Thomas S.D. - August 22, 1982) (E. Roy Ward photo)

Power for the Parsons - Dailey - Belington local leaves the engine terminal to make up his train at Elkins. WM was one of a few railroads that had low-hood Geeps. June 9, 1975. (E. Roy Ward photo)

Train time at Elkins. A Laurel Bank extra prepares to leave for Laurel Bank. October 12, 1984. (E. Roy Ward photo)

The rear end of an eastbound train along the Shavers Fork at milepost C16 on the GC&E S.D. May 8, 1977. (E. Roy Ward photo)

A Laurel Bank extra pulls through a 25° curve near Mt. Airy on the GC&E S.D. June 19, 1977. (E. Roy Ward photo)

A Laurel Bank extra east along the Shavers Fork at Crouch Run, W. Va. August 2, 1978. (E. Roy Ward photo)

A work extra picking up scrap on the GC&E S.D. just east of Laurel Bank, W. Va. October 14, 1985. (E. Roy Ward photo)

A Laurel Bank extra west's mid-train helper at Spruce, W. Va., swinging around the lower part of the horseshoe curve at Spruce. The head end of the train is on the 3% grade here and is approaching "Big Cut" at the summitt of Cheat Mountain at 4066 ft. above sea level. It is the highest common carrier railroad east of the Mississippi River. November 15, 1981. (E. Roy Ward photo)

Deep in Shavers Fork, a Laurel Bank extra west heads down the river on June 19, 1977. (E. Roy Ward photo)

A Laurel Bank switcher crew arrives at Bergoo from Webster Springs and prepares to switch Hylow Mine. The Laurel Bank switcher crew relieved the Laurel Bank extra crews at Laurel Bank and did the work west of there along the Elk River. (E. Roy Ward photo)

Laurel Bank extra west in the Shavers Fork. The great 1985 flood has scoured the river clean and track rebuilding is evident. July 16, 1987. (E. Roy Ward photo)

A Laurel Bank extra west, with empties, climbs out of Elkins on a 2% grade through the Isner Loop approaching Tunnel No. 1 through Cheat Mountain on the Durbin S.D. on October 12, 1984. This is a 3-unit helper cut in mid-train. (E. Roy Ward photo)

An eastbound Laurel Bank switcher with a mid-train 4-unit helper just out of sight lifts the first cut of a double from Laurel Bank to Spruce through a section of over 2% grade and 22° curves below Mt. Airy, W. Va. After the switcher crew returns to Laurel Bank, they will be recrewed by a Laurel Bank extra east crew which will take the second double up the mountain to Spruce and pick up the first cut and proceed to Elkins. October 18, 1981. (E. Roy Ward photo)

The Laurel Bank extra west is about 3 miles below Cheat Bridge, W. Va., on July 11, 1980, as it winds its way up the Shavers Fork on WM's GC&E S.D. with empty hoppers for Elk River mines. Those eight engines on the head end will be split evenly between pullers and helpers on the return trip east. (E. Roy Ward photo)

A Laurel Bank extra west on the Durbin S.D. at Faulkner, W. Va., on October 12, 1984. (E. Roy Ward photo)